My 11 Plus Journey

By Oby Thompson

To my children and husband for their
love and support

Table of Contents

Contents

Chapter 1

Preparation

'Michael, it is time to get ready for Saturday school,' I said, shaking him gently. I heard a groan and watched as my 11 year old son tried to shake himself out of sleep. I immediately felt guilty for waking him so early on a Saturday morning, especially when his siblings were still sleeping.

I stood back and wondered if it is worth it- sending your children to grammar school. I could just easily sit back and wait for Michael to be allocated a place in the nearest secondary school come Match 3rd.

I subconsciously reconsidered all the schools in my area, their achievements and positions in the schools' league table and decided that a grammar school is the best alternative for my son.

If only the government could make the standard of all state schools the same as that of the selective/grammar schools, no parent, especially me would be going through this trouble. I would rather spend my Saturday morning in bed.

11 Plus tests are the route to gaining admission into selective and grammar schools.

It is the bane of contention for parents like me who have to pay to get their children ready for the tests.

I was wondering how my husband and I will pay for the next batch of lessons when I heard Michael whisper, 'Do I have to go'? Again, guilt tugged at my guts. I strengthened up and weakly said, 'Yes baby, you have to go.'

Flurry of activities followed. While Michael showered, I went downstairs to prepare breakfast for him and the whole family.

Shortly after 9am, we left the house to get to the centre for a 9.30am start. As I negotiated my car into the small car park of the church hall where the lesson is held every week, I saw other parents, some looking less pleased for being out this early, others smiling encouragement to their children. I kissed Michael and waved him off. The lesson will last for four hours.

This has been our routine for the past six months. You have to do this otherwise you are not giving your child the best opportunity to pass the test.

Many parents go though financial and emotional trauma to ensure that their children get the best possible education.

My husband and I are no different. Sometimes the impact on the family especially the child could be profound.

11 Plus tutorials are an expensive exercise, sometimes setting parents back £400 per month depending on the tutor or the tutorial centre. Somehow parents find the money to pay for these lessons.

Sometimes when I analyse the range of work the children have to cover for the tests, especially mathematics, it makes me cringe. It also makes me wish that I had paid more attention to my mathematics lessons at school.

What about verbal and non verbal reasoning? I seriously cannot get my head around some the questions.

I know some parents find themselves in the same position.

This is why sending your child to an expert tutor becomes very imperative.

'Who sets these questions'?

Who decides that one type of school is better than others simply because you have to sit a bunch of tests to get in? I pondered as I drove away to carry out other Saturday chores.

Practical tips:

1. Ask yourself if this is what you want for your child. There is a wealth of information in related websites to help you with your decision. I found www.11plus.co.uk and www.Chuckra.co.uk very helpful.

2. Arm yourself with information about the test- at least enough to explain it to your child. Some parents struggle to explain how the 11 Plus works and how to prepare their children for the tests.

3. Read comments and feedbacks by parents. The websites are full of them.

Chapter 2

Another Saturday, another lesson!

'Mummy my head hurts'. I heard Michael's voice as if in a trance. A gentle hand on my arm made me snap out of sleep. 'Oh baby, come here. Are you okay?' I heard myself ask before I could stop myself. He had just told me he had a headache. Of course he is not okay. 'Why do people react this way to situations like this?' I pondered as I gathered him into my arms, whispering soothingly. Needless to say that there was no Saturday school for him after that.

Michael suffers from migraines, a condition he has had for a couple of years. To date, we cannot explain why he developed migraines at the age of 9 years.

He has been admitted into hospital on two occasions in the past year. The headaches meant that his attendance at school had suffered over the years. Doctors certainly do not have any answers to our numerous questions. While some think it is migraine, others suggest it could be cluster headaches. They however agree on one thing though; that he would grow out of it. I can't wait, because there is nothing worse than watching your child suffer and knowing that there is nothing you can do to bring him relief. I often wish I could take the headaches from him, and one day I said that to Michael. It broke my heart when he said, 'Mummy no one deserves to suffer from these headaches'. I cried for days after that.

Anyway, I proceeded to make Michael comfortable for the morning.

I also called the tutor to inform her that Michael would not attend school that morning.

As Michael went back to sleep, I went downstairs for a much needed cup of black coffee. As I sipped my coffee, staring absent-mindedly out of the kitchen window, I silently prayed that this latest bout of headaches would not result to a full blown migraine, which could last for days. Unfortunately, the Consortium of Selective Schools in Essex (CSSE) had brought the test date closer by a month.

While the test was previously in October, it is now in September. This is not ideal as it means that the school syllabus in English and mathematics are not often completed before the tests.

I know other parents are upset about this because it means extra work for the children and more spending by parents to get the extra work covered by the 11 Plus tutors.

After my coffee I decided to go food shopping, leaving instructions for my husband to look after Michael's wellbeing.

In the middle of my shopping I felt my phone vibrate. I took it out of my pocket and stared at the screen. It was my friend, Una, from South Africa.

We met and became friends during one of our children's many school trips.

Her daughter is the same age as Michael. Una is a wonderful person, but also one of the most paranoid people I have ever known. She sees conspiracy in everything.

Una would talk over you; go through discussions in seconds without taking a breath, and certainly without letting me provide answers to her numerous questions. 'If you know the answer to everything Una, why call to ask me?' I asked her one day.

Finally, with one hand on the trolley, I answered the phone and exhaled deeply at the first question. At least this is one question I can answer.

It turns out that she wanted the list of books her daughter can use in preparation for the 11 plus tests. 'Why don't you try these?' I listed the Bond series; Bond English 11-12 years, Bond Maths 10-11 and 11-12, Bond verbal and non verbal reasoning. Why don't you try the Collins series?' I asked.

I could hear Una making deep noises with her throat as if she was being strangled. 'Una', I shouted down the phone. 'Are you listening'? She shouted back, 'Where will I get the money to buy all these books?' She asked. 'I pay for school meals, music tuition, pay for everything, now this. This is ridiculous'. She concluded, breathing heavily in anger and frustration.

I reminded her that applying to a selective/grammar school is a matter of choice.

She grunted. She would have none of this argument.

'Why can't the government put money into the local schools to make them more attractive choices for parents? That would save us the trouble and agony of 11 Plus tests,' she moaned.

Many parents I have spoken to, share the same sentiment.

But that is a matter for another day and time. Finally, I directed her to WH Smith, to buy the books.

'You seem to know what you are saying, please come with me,' she said, but I made my excuses and ended the conversation.

Most parents are confused about the 11 Plus assessment, especially with the amount of work the children have to cover, the frequency of studies and the books to buy.

I have found that it is always helpful to talk to other parents with similar experience or whose children have taken the test in the past.

There is also a wealth of experience to be found in the internet, especially with support groups. Beware! The information can be very daunting.

Some information may leave you feeling inadequate with the study plan you have set out for your child.

With some parents, entry into a grammar school for their children is a battlefield situation. They start preparing their children about four years before the test, hire home tutors, and spend hundreds of pounds buying books. Some situations can be extreme but the importance of preparation cannot be over emphasised.

Bear in mind that many grammar schools have different 'cut off' marks and are very competitive; therefore in order to get into those schools, even more work is required by your child.

Schools like Dartford Grammar school for Boys, Dartford Grammar School for Girls; both in Kent, King Edward Grammar School, Southend High school for Boys and Southend High school for Girls both in Essex are highly competitive and receive hundreds of applications each year from parents in priority and out of priority areas.

This is the same for many grammar schools and selective schools in many Boroughs and Counties across the country. Tiffin Girls and Tiffin Boys in Surrey are worth considering, depending on where you live.

No matter where you live, the competition for places is high indeed!

Grays in Essex where we live is a small town, although the largest town in Thurrock. Many years ago, when my daughter, Georgia sat the test, it was just her and two other children in her primary school who sat the test.

However, in recent years, Grays has seen an influx of people, bringing the attendant oversubscription in primary and secondary schools in the area and surrounding areas.

As Grays does not have grammar or selective schools, many parents have therefore been forced to travel far to seek better education for their children.

Today, it gives me great joy to see boys and girls with their green uniform ensemble at Grays station in the morning, heading off to either Southend High School for Boys or Southend High School for Girls. Many parents have also resorted to private school education.

Practical Tips:

1. Make a decision as to how far you want your child to travel to school.

2. Then make a decision about the schools you would like to apply to.

3. Register your child for lessons early. Some parents start about two or three years before the test.

4. Encourage your child to read a book a week. Start your child on simple

books, and then move to more dense books as they grow older. This will help and improve their vocabulary and understanding of comprehension exercises.

5. Encourage your child to read to you for twenty minutes at least three times a week and discuss difficult words and sentences.

6. Make time to encourage your child and be prepared to help them through difficult questions. Ask other members of the family to help where you can't. My first son would often step in to help Michael with mathematics, while Georgia helped with English and verbal reasoning. Make it a team effort. It is worth it.

7. Choose the right tutorial centre for your child. Don't just go to any centre.

A bit of research of centres in your area will save you money and disappointment. Some of them are opportunists and only want your money. Pay visits to the centres before making your decision. Find out how many children they have helped secure grammar school places in the last five years. Find out the qualification of the tutors and their experiences with 11 Plus tests. Chances are, if they know what they are doing, with hard work your child will score high marks and could gain a grammar school place.

8. Encourage your child by paying attention to his/her questions and uncertainties. Praise him/her often. Children do well when their hard work is recognised and appreciated. Don't we all?

Chapter 3

Kent Tests
Practice Test Day 8 September

'Wake up baby'. I prodded Michael gently.

The previous day was very busy in my house, with my older children, Oj and Georgia quizzing Michael to see if he was ready for the test.

Michael took everything in his stride, looking from one person to another, nodding his head and answering their questions.

We had spent most of the day going through non verbal and verbal reasoning papers.

I was particularly worried about mathematics, but Michael assured me that he was 'on top of it'.

He must have gone through most of the books on mathematics in the stores. You would think that with all the preparation, I would be confident. Right? Wrong! I was so stressed. My stomach was all knotted up. I felt sick. I was still stressing when I sent Michael to sleep at 9pm.

'Mummy, should I wake up now?' Michael said rubbing his eyes with his knuckles.

It was 7am. The test centre, Invicta Grammar school for Girls is about fifty minutes from Grays. We therefore had to make an early start. I gently led Michael to the bathroom to have a quick shower.

While I was making breakfast, I called my friend and neighbour Nina, whose son, CJ was also sitting the same tests. We had decided to take one car and Nina would be driving.

As we finally drove off, with the children's packed lunches safely in the boot, I prayed that both boys will be alert to the questions as they can be very tricky. Such a burden to place on such young shoulders! I sighed as I listened to the chirpy voice of the satnav direct us to our destination. We all released a collective sigh of relief when we arrived at the test centre with thirty minutes before start time.

We secured our packing space, and watched as other parents drove in and packed their cars. We equally watched as the children shrieked in delight as they recognised their friends from various schools.

Fifteen minutes later, with the children registered and settled, I explained to the examiner about Michael's headaches. She made a note and promised to look out for him in case he developed headaches during the test.

Finally, the examiners ushered all the parents out of the room. We then decided to go to the shopping centre to wait. 'Why not'? I mused. The test will last for about four hours. Enough time to eat, shop and exchange our experiences about 11 plus.

As we finally settled down at the local McDonald's restaurant, some parents regaled us with stories about the preparation they had gone through with their children. Some of the tales made me feel like our preparations for Michael were insufficient, and we had had a lot!

It is important to stress that passing the tests is not enough. It is the first step. Your child has to score sufficiently high enough to fall within the required intake for the school year, which is usually between one hundred and twenty to one hundred and fifty children, depending on the school and its resources.

Therefore, coming from Grays which is a non priority area, makes it even difficult as the successful candidates from the Kent area were likely to be considered ahead of candidates from other areas.

Gulping my now lukewarm cappuccino, I told myself not to worry as there was nothing to be gained from worrying at this time.

Hours later, test over, we watched as the children were ushered out to their parents, some smiling, some pensive. How will Michael look? I finally spied him at the back, looking up to find me.

He was smiling. Hurray! At least he does not have a headache. I was very relieved to see his smiling face.

'Mummy, it was easy!' He pulled at my hand, still smiling.

Relief! I immediately wanted to know everything, but I restrained myself. There was no need to make him relive it just yet.

As we filed out to our various cars; we waved our goodbyes to other parents and children. I heard one parent say, 'See you next week'.

This was just the practice test. Kent council and maybe some other local authorities hold a practice test session, a week before the actual test.
I think this is the best practice as it enables the candidates familiarise themselves with what to expect on the actual test day.

The same flurry of activities took place a week later at the same test centre.

This time, it was the actual test. Sure enough, I saw the same parents. Again, Michael thought the tests were easy.

Again I wanted him to tell me about the test, the questions and all. But I restrained myself. As we drove home, I heard Michael and CJ discussing football. Very typical! Many adults would have been recounting the detail of the test and wondering how they did.

Practical Tips:

1. Send your child early to bed on the night before the test.

2. Ensure you arrive at the test centre early as arriving late is likely to destabilise your child and put him/her at a disadvantage.

3. Take advantage of practice tests where offered. It will help your child. It will give your child better perspective about the test in general.

4. Find practice test centres in the internet for the centres close to you. Be prepared to travel out of your Borough for practice tests where you cannot find one in your area.

Chapter 4

Essex Test Day
20 September

Just like the Kent tests before this, practices of test papers dominated our lives in the days leading to this day. I thought it will never end. You can only imagine how Michael felt and I imagine most children taking the tests must have felt the same way.

Michael had suffered a reoccurrence of headaches. I silently prayed that it would not rear its ugly head today. Michael had woken up before I went to his room.

I was not sure I liked this as it is often a red flag that his headache was imminent. My heart skipped and I looked deep into his eyes as if wanting to see the headache and take it out of him.

'Are you okay baby?' He nodded and went into the bathroom.

'God help us today,' I prayed silently.

After the attendant flurry of activities, we again drove with my friend Nina and her son CJ to Westcliff Grammar School for Boys, which was the designated test centre for Michael.

CJ was to sit his test at Southend Grammar School for Boys. Luckily, both schools are close to each other. On the way, I kept sneaking glances at Michael who was unusually quiet. I knew he was not worried about the test because I knew that he was prepared. He had given it his best.

At the test centre, I made sure to tell the examiners about Michael's headache in case there was a problem during the test.

We left for the town centre for another bout of shopping and chit chats. Some parents we met at Kent were also at the town centre. Again, we sat at the local McDonald's. We chatted and waited.

Hours later, as we all waited to collect the children; I became worried that it had taken more time than expected for Michael to come out.

Finally, I spied him at the back looking forlorn and downcast. Watching him standing there, clutching his pencil case tightly to his chest broke my heart. There was no doubt that his headache had resurfaced during the test. He had worked so hard these past months only for him to have a bad test day. As I approached him, he started crying and my eyes welled up with tears.

'My poor baby, what happened?' I asked.

'My head and tummy hurt, I had to go to the medical room for a while'. Michael said in a shaky voice.

I scooped him into my arms while he sobbed out his frustration and obvious anger that his headache and tummy had intervened in what would have otherwise been a good test day.

Situations like this could never be predicted. I tried to calm him down and led him to the waiting car, where he promptly fell asleep.

Practical Tips:

1. If your child has a medical condition, notify the appropriate test board with doctor's letter or medical report well before the test day.

2. Notify the examiners on the day of the test and provide your phone number

and stay within reach in case you have to go and collect your child urgently.

3. Your child may have the opportunity to sit the test on a different day if he is taken ill on the day or before the day, but you must provide a medical report and inform the test board on time.

4. If your child falls ill on test day, contact the relevant test board by email and follow it up with a phone call. It might not tip the scale in your child's favour but it may be taken into consideration during the appeal process, if you have to go through appeal.

5. If your child suffers a mishap on the test day, ensure that he/she does not blame himself/herself. While we

believe that children are resilient, and often forget such mishaps in no time, they also often internalise them and remain worried and confused for a long time.

6. Talk to your child and encourage your child to talk about what happened.

Chapter 5

Kent Results Day

What is it with parents who panic at everything? I panic whenever my children are sitting any tests or examination. Although I try not to show it in case I transfer my panic to them, they often see it and eventually end up reassuring me. Am I the one sitting the tests? No. But I panic anyway. Today was certainly no different; for today we receive the Kent test assessment result. I called a few parents who shared my anxiety and discussed the test all over again.

I must have checked my email a thousand times but finally, at around 16.20, my email pinged. I hesitated before I opened the message.

With a pounding heart, I read, *'Please be advised that Michael has been assessed suitable for admission to a Kent grammar school'*. I was ecstatic. I immediately called Michael. He was very happy, but he wanted to know his score. I did too because that would tell us whether he scored high enough to make the one hundred and twenty or so pupils who will gain admission to a Kent grammar school. But I did not have the scores at this time. For now though I rejoiced that the first huddle has been crossed. I prayed silently for other parents like me who will be opening their emails to the news.

One down, one to go!

I sat back and wondered what the Essex Test Assessment result will be. 'You will find out in a few days,' I told myself.

Practical Tips:

1. As soon as you get the good news, read the accompanying information thoroughly to see what steps you need to take next.

2. Equip yourself with information about cut off marks, especially of previous years and number of intakes for your preferred schools

3. Praise and show your child how proud you are.

Chapter Six

October -Essex Test Assessment Result day

Again, my anxiety peaked. But this time, not for long. Michael again passed the assessment. We were all very happy, especially given that he did not finish the test due to his headache on the day. In fact, he scored reasonably high. His score was 324.75 points. While Michael and the rest of my family were happy, I was worried that he may not have made the mark required for children from out of priority areas like Grays. At this stage, we did not know what the cut off mark would be.

Anyway, as parents have the right to express a preference for the school they want their child to attend, we decided to choose Westcliffe High School for Boys, Southend High School for Boys, Dartford Grammar School and Wilmington Grammar School for Boys in that order.

As The Education Act 1996 as amended by the Education and Inspections Act 2006 gives us parents the right to make preferences and the right for them to be met, we prayed that come March 3rd, one of our preferences will be offered to Michael. Well, 'providing that to do so would not prejudice the provision of efficient education, or efficient use of resources'.

Practical Tips:

1. Praise your child, whether he/she has passed the tests or not.

2. For those who did not pass, gently tell them and reassure them. It is not time for recrimination, especially if you as a parent did not start your child's preparation on time.

3. Before choosing your preferred schools, be realistic about your child's score. Find out the cut off mark for each school for previous years and decide whether your child has any realistic chance of getting an offer.

4. Decide how far you think it is practicable and reasonable for your child to travel before choosing the school. Always consider the cost of travel to and from the schools of your choice. Local authorities may not fund travel to grammar schools which are outside their Boroughs.

5. Spend some time researching your preferred schools. Schools' open evenings are good opportunities to find out important information about the particular school you are interested in. If you did not attend the open evening, call the school and arrange a visit. Most schools are flexible that way.

6. Visit the websites. Most schools' websites are user friendly and most information can be assessed this way. If not, make enquiries of the school, especially of their bullying policy.

7. Contact parents who already have children in your preferred schools. You will find their experiences and information they will share invaluable.

Chapter 7

March 3rd - School Notification Day

Again, I am all knotted up inside. Will Michael be allocated one of our preferred schools? I wondered, as I sat in front of my computer at work imagining what information I will find when next I hear my email ping. I worried even more when I remembered that we had not chosen any non Grammar school near us as a backup.

I was rudely shaken out of my deep thoughts by the dull ringing of my phone. I had chosen this tone to avoid my phone disturbing the rest of the office. To date, I still wonder why I do not like to leave my phone on vibrate. If the truth be told, I hate the sound it makes on my office table.

Anyway, I snatched the phone off my desk as soon as I realised that it was my sister, Ngozi, calling. Now, I do not hesitate in saying that my sister is the best sister in the world. My pain is her pain, my anxiety is her anxiety. She lends a listening ear whenever I want to complain about the inadequacies of the school system, even when she has her own worries and problems to deal with. Needless to say, that she understood the importance of this day.

'Hello, hello'. I heard my sister's authoritative voice demanding my attention. Before she could go any further, I said, 'I have not heard anything'. I said. She sighed and said, 'Well, let me know as soon as you know, bye'. Shortly afterwards, I received the notification via email. 'You were not allocated one of your preferred schools'. I dropped my phone so hard on my work table it rattled.

Oh dear! After all said and done, Michael was not given a place in one of our chosen schools!

The agony of it all! Work was a blur after that. I didn't know how to tell my husband. And I knew he was equally anxious as was Michael. Everybody would be gutted.

Home at last!

Try breaking important news with the expectant and hopeful eyes of your family on you. Very scary! Trust me!

I finally told them. Michael started to cry. My husband's face was a picture of disappointment. My eyes clouded over. My heart was in shreds. How do you explain to your child that although he passed all the tests, he did not secure a place in any of his chosen schools?

Pure agony!

I finally calmed everybody down. My husband leant a voice of reasoning like he always does when I get so angry and ready to give up, for right then, I wanted to give up especially as my son was hurting so badly. Now, Michael has no school that we want him to go to. What next?

Practical Tips:

1. Reassure your child.

2. Activate your plan B. You must have a plan B; otherwise you will struggle to immediately find a solution or an option you may wish to explore.

Chapter 8

Appeals Process

Appealing the decision not to offer your child a place in your preferred schools can often be very stressful and daunting. Some people see the process as draconian. Some parents I spoke to told me they would most definitely not appeal the decision not to offer their children places in their preferred schools. Who is to blame them? I can see why they may think this way. My good friend, Una, told me that the process is like giving a sweet to a child and then taking it away immediately. On one hand, the appeal papers are telling you that the school is oversubscribed, and on the other hand, inviting you to make your case, telling them why you think that the school should offer your child a place in a school where they already have their complete quota for the year.

Anyway, we decided that the best thing was to appeal to all four schools we choose. What choice did we have? Michael did not have a suitable school to go come September, and we were determined to give grammar school another go.

Firstly, we researched the websites of our preferred schools for information on how to appeal and the deadlines by which our appeal must be submitted. All local authorities have different deadlines for appeals, so we started with Essex County.

For Westcliff High School for Boys, we were required to make our representations to the Admission Authority, enclosing our appeal statement, reports from medical experts regarding Michael's headaches and letter from St Thomas of Canterbury Primary

School Grays, regarding Michael's academic performance. Westcliff High School for Boys of course, for the appeal, submitted the *'School Statement to the panel incorporating its policy for admission to the school at age 11'*. After many months of waiting to hear our appeal, the appeal panel considered the submissions of the Admissions Authority and summarised among other statements that *'Under the 1998 School Standards and Framework Act (as amended by the Education and Inspections Act 2006) to admit Michael would prejudice the provision of efficient education or the efficient use of resources in that to admit in excess of 154 pupils in year seven would be detrimental to the efficient provision of education'*. The Panel went further to consider the appeal under the 'group stage' and concluded that it was '---satisfied that to admit further students would prejudice the effective delivery of education at the school'*.

The Panel was then faced with considering our submissions and deciding whether the decision of the Admission Authority should be overturned.

The Panel conceded among many reasons given, that *'Michael had scored some way above the pass mark for the tests so there was no question as to his ability'.*

That notwithstanding, the Panel was *'satisfied that prejudice to the provision of efficient education and the efficient use of resources, as defined in section as defined in section 86 paragraph 3 (a) & (c) of the School Standards and Framework Act 1998, would result if your child were admitted to the school, namely that although his result indicated that Michael is of grammar school standard he had failed to achieve the required mark to be offered a place as an out of "preferred area" student and his admission would be incompatible with the School's admission arrangement. In addition the school will be oversubscribed. The Panel was not satisfied that your reasons for wishing your child to be admitted to the school were sufficient to outweigh this and accordingly decided not to allow your appeal'.*

How do you continue in the face of their argument? While we want our children to attend grammar schools, we also have to recognise or appreciate the fact that the school may indeed be oversubscribed and that this could indeed be detrimental to our children's learning.

I also sympathise with the school as it struggles to create a fair and reasonable balance between what the available resources can provide and the children's well being.

Needless to say that while we may understand the reasons for the decision, we were again gutted by yet another decision not to give Michael a place at a grammar school.

The appeal to Southend Grammar School for Boys followed almost the same pattern, but this time, we had to appeal directly to the Headmaster, with the same submissions as we did with Westcliff High School for Boys. Again, the outcome was devastating. We had decided to keep Michael in the dark about the various appeals. We did not want to disappoint him again. All I could say to his endless questions about which school he would be attending, was 'we are working at it'. Not particularly reassuring, but we were indeed working at it. I had in the interim applied to St Thomas More Primary school Westcliff on-Sea as our plan B.

Chapter 9

Kent Appeals

The appeal process for Kent Admission was very much the same as that of Essex County and I believe with pretty much other local authorities.

Again, we sent our representations and argued our reasons why we thought Michael should be given a place at Dartford Grammar School for Boys. The appeal day was conducted on two stages, with the school giving its submission to all the parents, which my husband thought was very discouraging, as any parent present would have been forgiven for thinking that the school was immediately telling you not to bother with the appeal as their minds were already made up; you will not be successful!

Anyway, with only my beloved husband in attendance during the individual appeal session, I fretted while at work until he called to say it was finished and that 'we should keep our fingers crossed'. My husband is a very persuasive speaker and I decided that if anybody could convince the Panel, he would. This was now our third appeal and our hopes were wearing thin. My anxiety level had peaked to an abnormal level at this time.

Lo and behold, a few days later, came a letter from Clerk to the Appeal Panel with the now much dreaded news. The Panel noted that *'an older brother is in 6th Form; Michael has a medical condition of recurrent headaches and had a headache during the Kent Test. However, it was felt that these were not sufficiently strong for them to make an exception in this case'*.

Sweet Lord! What else could they want? I tried to rationalise the situation. At this stage, it is easy to be uncharitable and blame the school for not giving my son a place. Do I really want my son to be another number in an already oversubscribed school? Am I really looking out for his wellbeing? When you are desperate for your child to gain admission into a grammar school, it is hard to put things into perspective. I am sure the various grammar schools would want to give a place to every deserving applicant, but do they have the resources for it?

Our last and final appeal was directly to Wilmington Grammar School Kent. After much discussion with my husband, we decided that that the outcome was more likely to be the same as the previous three. We therefore decided not to attend the appeal hearing. We contacted the school and asked the Panel to consider our appeal in our absence. At this point we had decided that Michael would be going to St Thomas More anyway, and told him so. We had put things in place for that but we were hedging our bet on buying the uniform, just in case some miracle happened.

And it did!

Wilmington Grammar for Boys had come through for us. They considered our representations albeit in our absence, and decided that Michael should be offered a place in the school. We were ecstatic! Michael was jumping all over the house. He was very happy that his efforts had finally paid off.

I immediately contacted the school and registered our acceptance of the offer. I also cancelled our acceptance at St Thomas More to enable the school allocate that space to another child who may need it.

Our happiness did not end there. Just as we were about to embark on the journey of buying school uniforms for Michael, Southend High School for Boys called me. I remember that day very clearly. I was having my mid morning coffee at work when the call came through. When the voice at the end of the phone told me that the school was now offering Michael a place at the school, I was so shocked that I kept shouting, 'Really, oh my God' at the voice. I must have said it more than a dozen times before finally accepting the offer and hanging up the phone.

It was the best news in this admission process that started so unhappily for us. Now to be offered two grammar schools in one week was unbelievable.

At home that night Michael celebrated with his much loved KFC, while the rest of us celebrated with Chinese food.

Our acceptance of the offer of Southend Grammar School for Boys was very easy. While to this day we appreciate the consideration Wilmington Grammar School for Boys gave our appeal, travelling to Southend is much easier for Michael.

I am very happy that it turned out very well in the end for us. It was a roller coaster journey for us, what with Michael's illness, the money spent for lessons, the rejections and emotional highs and lows. Was it all worth it? Definitely yes! Southend High School for Boys is one of the best all round achieving schools in the country and we are happy to be associated with it!

Most importantly, Michael is happy and thriving in the school.

Practical Tips:

1. Do not be discouraged by the appeal process. It is there for a reason. Do not give up. Where your child has achieved a good mark, go for appeal.

2. Spend time researching the school's website as well as the Admission authorities' guidance for parents. Look at each school's oversubscription criteria and decide where your child falls into.

3. Prepare a very good appeal submission. Get somebody to help you if you do not know what to include in your submission. Chances are a well written argument may sway the panel into giving that one place to your child. Remember to include in your submission your child's sporting, musical and academic achievements. They may sway the appeal panel in your child's favour.

4. Most importantly, have a plan B. Apply to other local schools for a place pending the outcome of the appeal. More often, parents do not take up

places for their children for many reasons, leaving the school with places to offer new applicants.

5. Place your child's name on the waiting list of your preferred school. Such list often last for a year, or until you ask that your child's name be taken off the list.

6. If your appeal is not upheld, scrutinise the reasons given. If you believe that the Panel did not follow the correct procedures or did not act fairly and independently during the process, you can complain to the Education Funding Agency.

Chapter 10

Alternative to Grammar/Selective Schools

Many parents often think that private schools are for the rich and privileged few in the society. They shy away from the mere mention of private school education for their children. My friend Una certainly thought I was joking when I explained how she could put her child through private education without paying any fees.

While private schools may have been for the rich and privileged many years ago, the situation is different now.

The government is constantly inviting private schools to offer places to less privileged children, who would otherwise not be able to attend such schools.

If you are working, or even on welfare benefit, your child could benefit from private education. All your child has to do is pass the entrance tests for the particular school.

In fact, independent schools such as City of London School for Boys, City of London School for Girls, Chigwell School, St Alban's School, King's College School, Latymer Upper School, St Paul's Girls' School, St Paul's School, Westminster School, to mention a few, are always 'offering subsidized places to children who do well in their entrance exams, but whose parents might otherwise be unable to pay the fees'.

If your children are gifted in music, Arts or spots, they stand better chances of securing places.

So what are you waiting for? While the above schools might not be in your area, there may be independent schools in your Borough or close to you.

Practical Tips:

1. Equip yourself with information. Search for independent schools in your area. Visit the Independent Schools Council website for more information.

2. Identify the schools you want to apply to. Download past questions from the website and give to your child to attempt.

3. Arrange for extra lessons if you or anyone in the family would be unable to provide extra tutorials.

4. Make the necessary applications with correct fees where application fees are applicable.

Most importantly, and some people may find this advice extreme, move to the area with good schools. This was not the advice we had given ourselves when we were looking to move house. All we cared about was that we would be buying a home in a relatively affordable area. We did not factor into it the fact that we will be commuting to London for work. A very expensive exercise! We did not also factor into it the fact that we will be paying for school transport for our children, especially when it transpired that school children in London do not pay bus fares. Unless you are a very high earner, you have not really made any savings if you moved the way we did.

Don't get me wrong, I love Grays, especially since it provided us with the perfect environment to raise three wonderful children in relative peace.

I do not however blame parents who move house because of good schools. If you are as passionate about education as I am, you will consider it!

Printed in Great Britain
by Amazon.co.uk, Ltd.,
Marston Gate.